CONTENTS

CHAPTER 1: A CHILDHOOD PAINTED IN FAITH AND LOVE

Ah, my childhood in Jamaica was a masterpiece of faith and love, a tapestry woven with threads of devotion and sacrifice. Our family, led by my hard-working parents, breathed the essence of Christianity into our daily lives (Proverbs 22:6). I was one of seven children, the second boy and the third oldest, and our home was a lively haven of love and activity.

Sundays were sacred days for us, a time when our entire family gathered to attend the local church together. Despite the occasional internal struggles and rivalries within the congregation, I found solace in the fellowship and sense of community it provided (Hebrews 10:25). There, I discovered kindred spirits who shared the same beliefs and values.

But faith knew no boundaries for us; it thrived beyond the church walls. In our home, a beautiful tradition unfolded – prayer meetings that brought us even closer. Our hearts entwined as we sang hymns and lifted up each other's needs and concerns in prayer (James 5:16). Those intimate moments not only fortified our family bond but also deepened our connection with God.

Yet, amid all our religious practices, we still revelled in the simple joys of childhood. My siblings and I would engage in delightful games, crafting memories that would be etched in our hearts forever. Our home echoed with the melodies of songs and the laughter of innocence (Psalm 100:1-2). Even fetching water from the nearby river during water shortages became an adventure, a chance to marvel at nature's beauty and acknowledge the blessings bestowed upon us (Psalm 104:24).

Through it all, our faith was the bedrock of our lives, the anchor that steadied us. We believed in the power of prayer (Mark 11:24) and sought guidance from Jesus in every aspect of our existence (Proverbs 3:5-6). Our love for one another mirrored the love that Jesus had for us, and we leaned on each other for unwavering support (John 13:34-35).

As the years passed, my appreciation for the role I played in our close-knit family only deepened. We were not just a group of relatives – we were a living family, interconnected by shared beliefs and an unbreakable bond of love (1 Corinthians 12:12-13). Together, we faced life's highs and lows, celebrating each triumph and offering comfort during moments of sorrow (Romans 12:15).

Reflecting on my cherished childhood, I am overwhelmed with gratitude for the solid foundation of faith and love that my parents bestowed upon us. It has shaped me into the person I am today, someone who holds family, community, and a profound connection with God in the highest regard (Deuteronomy 6:6-7).

Now, as I embark on this journey to recount my experiences, my heart brims with thankfulness. My childhood of faith and love has set the stage for the chapters yet to come. Among them, I anticipate moments of sheer joy, formidable challenges, and, above all, an even deeper understanding of the unwavering power of faith and the boundless love that emanates from Jesus (Romans 8:38-39). I invite you to join me on this voyage, where the brushstrokes of faith will paint vivid pictures of life's profound mysteries.

CHAPTER 2:
BATTLING DARKNESS
AND DESPAIR

High school can be a treacherous battleground. It's a place where insecurities are magnified, and the weight of the world seems to rest on your shoulders. For me, this chapter of my life was filled with darkness and despair, as I battled against the formidable foes of depression, rejection, and spiritual wickedness.

In those hallways, the whispers of self-doubt and worthlessness echoed relentlessly, drowning out any glimmer of hope. Every day felt like an uphill struggle, a fight to keep my head above water and find a sense of belonging in a sea of judgemental eyes. The weight of expectations suffocated me as if the world's burden was crushing my spirit.

Yet, in the midst of the chaos and anguish, I discovered a lifeline, a beacon of hope in the midst of the storm - my Christian faith. In those moments of deep despair, I clung to the promises of God, finding strength in His words and the knowledge that I was not alone. The verses from Psalms and Isaiah became my refuge, providing solace and courage to face each day.

Rejection became an unwelcome companion, leaving me feeling isolated and unwanted. Friendships shattered, dreams crumbled, and it felt as though I was constantly being pushed aside. However, my faith taught me that my worth was not defined by the opinions of others. I held onto the truth that I was fearfully and wonderfully made and that God had a plan for my life, even if it seemed obscured in those dark moments.

But it wasn't just the struggles of everyday life that I faced; I also battled against unseen forces of spiritual wickedness. It felt as though malevolent powers were determined to extinguish the flickering flame of hope within me. However, I refused to let the darkness consume me. My Christian beliefs became my shield, and I found strength in prayer, seeking refuge in the loving embrace of my Heavenly Father.

This chapter of my life was undoubtedly one of the hardest I had ever faced. High school struggles tested my resilience and challenged my faith. But through it all, I emerged stronger, with a renewed sense of purpose. I learned to trust in God's plan, even when it seemed impossible to see the light at the end of the tunnel. The verse from Romans became my anchor, assuring me that God works all things for the good of those who love Him.

The battles I fought in those high school hallways may have left scars, but they also shaped me into the person I am today. They taught me the power of perseverance, the importance of leaning on my faith, and the resilience of the human spirit. As I turned the page to the next chapter of my life, I carried with me the lessons learned and the unwavering hope that comes from clinging to Christian beliefs.

The trials I faced in my youth only served to strengthen my resolve. I realized that life's hardships could not break me, for I was sustained by a faith that transcended all obstacles. With each step forward, I felt a profound connection to the divine, guiding me towards a purpose greater than myself.

Though the battles were fierce, and the nights seemed endless, I held onto hope, for hope was the anchor of my soul. Through the darkest valleys, I found courage, knowing that God's love was greater than any darkness seeking to engulf me. My faith was not a crutch; it was my unwavering foundation, upon which I built my resilience and determination.

As I stepped into the unknown of the next chapter, I knew that life would continue to test me. But I faced the future with newfound strength and the assurance that, no matter what lies ahead, I will walk through it with my head held high, for I am never alone. My Christian beliefs would be my guide, illuminating the path and dispelling the shadows.

And so, with my heart fortified by the wisdom gained through hardships, and my faith as the compass to navigate life's challenges, I embraced the journey ahead. For I knew that, armed with the teachings of my faith, I could face any darkness and despair that dared to cross my path. My story had just begun, and this chapter would be but a stepping stone toward the person I was destined to become.

CHAPTER 3: CROSSING BOUNDARIES: FROM JAMAICA TO LONDON IN 2002

As I take a moment to look back on that fateful decision that forever changed the course of my life – leaving behind the familiar and embarking on a journey to England – a profound sense of melancholy washes over me. The dreams that once burned bright with hope for a better future and a brighter tomorrow seemed to vanish into thin air as I set foot on foreign soil (Jeremiah 29:11 - "For I know the plans I have for you," declares the Lord, "plans to prosper you and not to harm you, plans to give you hope and a future.").

The clash with a new culture was a relentless torrent that threatened to smother my spirit. At every turn, I faced racism, classism, and prejudice, as if my mere existence was an inconvenience to those around me. My aspirations were shattered by a society that resisted embracing the diversity of my identity (James 2:1 - "My brothers and sisters, believers in our glorious Lord Jesus Christ must not show favouritism.").

Desperate to escape the harsh realities that engulfed me, I found myself ensnared in a web of immorality. The weight of depression bore down heavily, dragging me into a dark abyss of despair with each passing day. My relentless pursuit of employment yielded nothing but rejection and disappointment, leaving me jobless and disheartened (Psalm 34:17-18 - "The righteous cry out, and the Lord hears them; he delivers them from all their troubles. The Lord is close to the broken-hearted and saves those who are crushed in spirit.").

The living conditions in this vast city were deplorable, serving as a stark reminder of my perceived insignificance. With my pockets empty and my dreams distant, I struggled to make ends meet, barely scraping by on underpaid jobs that barely covered my basic needs. The burden of hopelessness weighed heavily on my shoulders, crushing my spirit and leaving me feeling utterly defeated (Matthew 6:26 - "Look at the birds of the air; they do not sow or reap or store away in barns, and yet your heavenly Father feeds them. Are you not much more valuable than they?").

Amid this tumultuous storm, I faced a heart-wrenching decision to walk away from my Christian faith. The pain and despair had led me to question the existence of a loving God. How could a benevolent deity allow such suffering? In my anguish, I felt abandoned, adrift in a world that seemed indifferent to my struggles (Psalm 13:1 - "How long, Lord? Will you forget me forever? How long will you hide your face from me?").

The dreams of pursuing education, once a beacon of ambition and motivation, came to an abrupt halt. The cycle of poverty that had haunted my family for generations seemed inescapable. Survival became my sole focus, leaving little room for aspirations or personal growth (Proverbs 16:3 - "Commit to the Lord whatever you do, and he will establish your plans.").

As I cast my gaze back on this poignant chapter of my life, a sense of melancholy envelopes me. The struggles I faced, the seemingly insurmountable adversity, have left indelible marks on my soul. The wounds may have healed, but the scars remain, a constant reminder of the hardships endured (2 Corinthians 4:8-9 - "We are hard pressed on every side, but not crushed; perplexed, but not in despair; persecuted, but not abandoned; struck down, but not destroyed.").

Yet, in the depths of darkness, I clung to a sliver of hope. There is more to this story – a tale of resilience, redemption, and the undying human spirit. Stay with me as I recount the chapters that follow, where I confront my inner demons, embrace the journey of self-discovery, and eventually emerge from the shadows to find the light of a new day.

CHAPTER 4: A DIVINE ENCOUNTER: EMBRACING THE LIGHT A MIDST DARKNESS

Amid the darkness that once threatened to engulf my life, a radiant ray of hope emerged, illuminating my path with divine intervention and God's infinite mercy and grace (Psalm 27:1 - "The Lord is my light and my salvation—whom shall, I fear? The Lord is the stronghold of my life—of whom shall I be afraid?").

It was on a momentous day, my birthday, that fate led me to encounter a beautiful woman who would later become my wife. From the very first moment, our connection felt destined, and little did I know that this meeting would herald a new chapter brimming with love and blessings (Proverbs 18:22 - "He who finds a wife finds what is good and receives favour from the Lord.").

Soon, the joyous news of her pregnancy filled our hearts with indescribable happiness. The prospect of becoming a father ignited a profound sense of purpose within me. This was a second chance, an opportunity to transform my life and create a brighter future for my growing family (Psalm 127:3 - "Children are a heritage from the Lord, offspring a reward from him.").

With renewed determination, I chose to return to the embrace of the church, despite my ongoing struggle with faith. There was a stirring within me, urging me to try again, to seek the connection I once had with God – the source of reassurance and guidance (James 4:8 - "Come near to God and he will come near to you. Wash your hands, you sinners, and purify your hearts, you double-minded.").

And then, a divine encounter changed everything. In the presence of God Himself, I felt enveloped by His love and mercy, a moment of profound clarity that reminded me I was never alone in my struggles. He had been with me all along, patiently waiting for me to reach out to Him (Isaiah 41:10 - "So do not fear, for I am with you; do not be dismayed, for I am your God. I will strengthen you and help you; I will uphold you with my righteous right hand.").

With this newfound faith, I witnessed positive changes unfurling in my life. I secured a better job, not necessarily the highest-paying one, but one that provided for my wife and our precious daughter. Financial stress began to dissipate, replaced by a sense of stability and security (Matthew 6:33 - "But seek first his kingdom and his righteousness, and all these things will be given to you as well.").

Hope returned, reigniting the desire to live a life of purpose. I left behind the immoral lifestyle that once ensnared me, instead focusing on building a strong and loving family. With my wife by my side, we embarked on a journey of growth, supporting and uplifting each other every step of the way (Ephesians 5:25 - "Husbands, love your wives, just as Christ loved the church and gave himself up for her.").

As I reflect on this profound chapter of my life, a deep sense of gratitude envelops me. The darkness that once threatened my soul has been replaced by a radiant light, guiding me toward a brighter future. Filled with hope and determination, I know that with

God's grace, anything is possible. Together, my family will forge ahead, rooted in love, faith, and unwavering resilience (Romans 15:13 - "May the God of hope fill you with all joy and peace as you trust in him, so that you may overflow with hope by the power of the Holy Spirit.").

CHAPTER 5: TOUCHED BY GRACE: EMBRACING HEALING THROUGH A DIVINE ENCOUNTER

Chapter 5: Touched by Grace: Embracing Healing through a Divine Encounter

The darkness that once enshrouded my life was on the brink of being shattered by an extraordinary touch from Jesus Himself – a touch filled with boundless compassion and power that promised to heal my brokenness, lift my depression, and liberate me from the afflictions that had held me captive for far too long (Psalm 34:18 - "The Lord is close to the broken-hearted and saves those who are crushed in spirit.").

Nights of despair had become my unwanted companions, as I sought solace under my pillow, trying to silence the relentless noise of my thoughts. The weight of depression made every sound an unbearable irritation, and I yearned for a glimmer of hope (Psalm 42:11 - "Why, my soul, are you downcast? Why so disturbed within me? Put your hope in God, for I will yet praise him, my Saviour, and my God.").

Yet, it wasn't only my mind that suffered; my body, too, was afflicted. The torment of acidity caused excruciating pain, leading me to frequent hospital visits. A stabbing sensation in my chest left me confined to a restrictive diet, as even a hint of fried or oily food would trigger unbearable agony. In one particularly distressing incident, an ambulance was summoned, and I found myself hooked up to a drip, praying for relief (Psalm 41:3 - "The Lord sustains them on their sickbed and restores them from their bed of illness.").

But amidst the physical and mental struggles, God was working behind the scenes, gently peeling away layers of anger, bitterness, pride, arrogance, malice, and lust that had entangled my soul. He was preparing me for an extraordinary encounter that would forever change my life (Ephesians 4:22-24 - "You were taught, with regard to your former way of life, to put off your old self, which is being corrupted by its deceitful desires; to be made new in the attitude of your minds; and to put on the new self, created to be like God in true righteousness and holiness.").

In the stillness of my room, I cried out to the Lord with profound frustration and sincere desperation. I implored Him to cleanse me of every unclean spirit and to fill me with the Holy Spirit's presence. Little did I know that this heartfelt plea would ignite a divine fire within my soul, a fire of the Holy Spirit that would consume the darkness and pave the way for a miraculous transformation (Luke 11:13 - "If you then, though you are evil, know how to give good gifts to your children, how much more will your Father in heaven give the Holy Spirit to those who ask him!").

From that pivotal moment, a tangible shift took hold of me. The oppressive weight of depression began to lift, making room for newfound peace and joy. The physical pain and acidity that once tormented my body gradually receded, as if the touch of Jesus Himself had brought about healing from within (Matthew 11:28-30 - "Come to me, all you who are weary and burdened, and I will give you rest. Take my yoke upon you and learn from me, for

I am gentle and humble in heart, and you will find rest for your souls. For my yoke is easy and my burden is light.").

As I continued to seek the Lord and surrender my life to Him, I encountered an overwhelming sense of His presence and love. His Word became a wellspring of comfort and guidance, and the fire of the Holy Spirit burned brighter within me with each passing day, empowering me to triumph over the struggles that once ensnared me (Psalm 119:105 - "Your word is a lamp for my feet, a light on my path.").

Reflecting on this pivotal chapter of my life, I am filled with awe and gratitude. Jesus, in His infinite mercy and compassion, touched my brokenness and ushered in healing and restoration. The journey was not without its challenges, but through His grace and power, I emerged stronger, embracing a life filled with hope, purpose, and unyielding faith (Psalm 103:2-5 - "Praise the Lord, my soul, and forget not all his benefits—who forgives all your sins and heals all your diseases, who redeems your life from the pit and crowns you with love and compassion, who satisfies your desires with good things so that your youth is renewed like the eagle's.").

As I venture forward, I carry with me the invaluable lessons learned during this transformative season. I now know that with Jesus by my side, no darkness can withstand the brilliance of His light, and through His touch, every part of my being is made whole.

CHAPTER 6: A MISSION FUELLED BY THE FIRE OF GOD

With the fire of God ablaze within me, my heart was engulfed in a newfound passion and purpose. I made a solemn vow to the Lord Jesus, promising that if He would anoint and equip me, I would dedicate my life to carrying His Gospel to the farthest reaches of the earth (Matthew 28:19-20 - "Therefore go and make disciples of all nations, baptising them in the name of the Father and of the Son and of the Holy Spirit, and teaching them to obey everything I have commanded you. And surely, I am with you always, to the very end of the age.").

Over the years, I've been privileged to witness His miraculous power at work as I shepherded Christ Liquid Fire Ministry in London. Our ministry became a beacon of hope, a haven where the broken-hearted found solace, the sick received healing, and the lost encountered the love of Jesus (Isaiah 61:1 - "The Spirit of the Sovereign Lord is on me because the Lord has anointed me to proclaim good news to the poor. He has sent me to bind up the broken-hearted, to proclaim freedom for the captives and release from darkness for the prisoners.").

The journey of pastoring this church has been an extraordinary mix of challenges and rewards. Through the ups and downs, God has remained faithful, guiding, and empowering me to be a vessel for His miracles, signs, and wonders. Witnessing blind eyes opening, deaf ears hearing, and the lame walking, the Holy Spirit has moved mightily in our midst, touching hearts, and transforming lives (Acts 10:38 - "How God anointed Jesus of Nazareth with the Holy Spirit and power, and how he went around doing good and healing all who were under the power of the devil because God was with him.").

But God's work hasn't been confined to our church walls. He has opened doors for me to conduct revivals and minister in various parts of the world. From America to Jamaica, and even throughout the United Kingdom, I've had the privilege of sharing the love and healing power of Jesus with people from all walks of life (Mark 16:15 - "He said to them, 'Go into all the world and preach the gospel to all creation.'").

In these revivals, I've witnessed the desperate cries of the lost, the broken, and the weary. Many have come burdened by pain and despair, seeking a glimmer of hope. It is in those poignant moments that I've experienced the undeniable presence of God, moving in hearts, and bringing about transformation (Psalm 34:17 - "The righteous cry out, and the Lord hears them; he delivers them from all their troubles.").

The testimonies of healing and deliverance are too numerous to count. I've seen cancerous tumours vanish, mental illnesses bow before the name of Jesus, and addictions shattered by His mighty hand. The power of God's love knows no bounds, and it's an incredible privilege to be a vessel through which He brings about His divine intervention (Jeremiah 32:27 - "I am the Lord, the God of all mankind. Is anything too hard for me?").

Yet, I recognize that these miracles do not happen through my strength or abilities. Instead, it is the Holy Spirit working through me, guiding my every step. I humbly understand that I am merely a vessel, surrendering myself to His will and allowing His power to flow through me (Zechariah 4:6 - "So he said to me, 'This is the word of the Lord to Zerubbabel: Not by might nor by power, but by my Spirit,' says the Lord Almighty.").

As I reflect on the journey thus far, I am both humbled by God's faithfulness and inspired by the tremendous responsibility of spreading His love and healing to a hurting world. I am reminded of the promise I made to the Lord, and I am deeply grateful for the opportunities He has granted me to fulfil that promise (Psalm 105:1 - "Give praise to the Lord, proclaim his name; make known among the nations what he has done.").

But the work is far from over. Countless souls still need redemption, broken hearts yearn for healing, and lives are waiting to be transformed by the power of Jesus. And so, I press on, fuelled by the fire of God within me, knowing that His love and power are limitless (Philippians 3:14 - "I press on toward the goal to win the prize for which God has called me heavenward in Christ Jesus.").

I am committed to continuing the work of spreading the Gospel, reaching out to the lost and broken, and being a vessel for God's miraculous touch. I will walk in obedience, trusting in His leading, and fully surrendering to His plans. For in His boundless love, there lies the power to heal and restore, and I am but an instrument of His grace in this magnificent symphony of redemption and hope.

CHAPTER 7: EMBRACING MERCY AND LOVE

As I sit here, reflecting on the remarkable journey of my life, I am overwhelmed by the immense mercy and love that Jesus has showered upon me. His grace has brought about a transformation so profound; I could never have imagined it on my own. Once shackled by the chains of depression, I now find solace in the loving arms of my Saviour, liberated from the grip of hopelessness and despair (Psalm 42:11 - "Why, my soul, are you downcast? Why so disturbed within me? Put your hope in God, for I will yet praise him, my Saviour and my God.").

My past was fraught with immorality and recklessness, but Jesus' boundless mercy granted me a second chance. Today, I am blessed with a loving spouse and the joy of a committed marriage. My transformation from sinner to pastor stands as a powerful testament to the redeeming power of Jesus' love (2 Corinthians 5:17 - "Therefore, if anyone is in Christ, the new creation has come: The old has gone, the new is here!").

Not only did Jesus heal my spiritual brokenness, but He also restored my physical health. Through His divine healing touch, I now lead a life filled with vitality and strength. The words from Psalm 103:2-3 echo deeply within me: "Bless the Lord, O my soul, and forget not all his benefits, who forgives all your iniquity, who heals all your diseases." I am living proof of God's healing power, and I shall forever praise Him for His boundless mercy and love (Matthew 8:17 - "This was to fulfil what was spoken through the prophet Isaiah: 'He took up our infirmities and bore our diseases.'").

Once, anger and bitterness consumed my heart, but Jesus' love has transformed me into a vessel of unconditional love. The wisdom of 1 John 4:7-8 resonates within me: "Beloved, let us love one another, for love is from God, and whoever loves has been born of God and knows God. Anyone who does not love does not know God, because God is love." Through Jesus' mercy, I have learned the art of forgiveness and the beauty of extending grace to others, just as He has done for me (Ephesians 4:31-32 - "Get rid of all bitterness, rage and anger, brawling and slander, along with every form of malice. Be kind and compassionate to one another, forgiving each other, just as in Christ God forgave you.").

Amidst rejection and the pain, it brings, I have witnessed Jesus' unyielding favour upon my life. In Psalm 30:5, it is written, "For his anger is but for a moment, and his favour is for a lifetime. Weeping may tarry for the night, but joy comes with the morning." Though others may have turned me away, I have found solace in the embrace of my Heavenly Father, who bestows His favour upon me abundantly (Romans 8:31 - "What, then, shall we say in response to these things? If God is for us, who can be against us?").

Lastly, I have beheld God's gracious provision in my life, lifting me from the depths of poverty and guiding me toward abundance. In Matthew 6:33, Jesus tells us, "But seek first the kingdom of God and his righteousness, and all these things will be added to you." Through His mercy and love, God has met my every need, reminding me that I am His beloved child (Philippians 4:19 - "And my God will meet all your needs according to the riches of his glory in Christ Jesus.").

In conclusion, my life stands as a living testimony to the mercy and love of Jesus Christ. His grace has liberated me from depression, immorality, sickness, anger, bitterness, rejection, and poverty. I am eternally grateful for His unwavering love and the hope He has bestowed upon me. May we all embrace His boundless grace and, in turn, share His overflowing mercy with the world (1 Peter 2:9 - "But you are a chosen people, a royal priesthood, a holy nation, God's special possession, that you may declare the praises of him who called you out of darkness into his wonderful light."). Let us be radiant beacons of His love, for the world to witness and be transformed by His mercy.

CHAPTER 8: CONQUERING THE SPIRIT OF FEAR

As I pen down this chapter, my heart overflows with reflections on the journey I've travelled. Fear has been a constant companion, stealthily lurking in the shadows, whispering lies that threaten to hinder my progress. The fears that have relentlessly haunted me the most are the fear of rejection, the fear of failure, and the fear of death.

Understanding the Grip of Fear

Fear is a formidable force, capable of paralysing us, robbing us of joy, and preventing us from embracing the abundant life God intended for us. The spirit of fear is a spiritual stronghold seeking to shatter our peace and obstruct our path to fulfilling God's purpose. Yet, I have learned that God has not bestowed this spirit upon us; instead, He has graced us with power, love, and a sound mind (2 Timothy 1:7).

Facing the Fear of Rejection

Amongst the fears that have most profoundly affected my life is the fear of rejection. Rooted in the yearning for acceptance and affirmation, it has hindered me from embracing my true self and pursuing my dreams. But along my journey, a truth became evident—I am not defined by the opinions of others; my identity and worth are firmly established in the unconditional love and acceptance of my Heavenly Father.

Conquering the Fear of Rejection with God's Unwavering Love

To vanquish the fear of rejection, I immersed myself in God's boundless love. Daily, I reminded myself that I am a marvellous creation, fearfully and wonderfully made (Psalm 139:14). I clung to scriptures that affirmed my identity in Christ, seeking solace in the community of believers who breathed life into my soul and reminded me of my inherent value.

Embracing Faith and Perseverance to Overcome the Fear of Failure

Another fear that imprisoned me was the fear of failure—the dread of inadequacy, the fear of faltering, and the pressure of unrealized expectations. Yet, I came to embrace failure as a gateway to growth and enlightenment, understanding that in my weaknesses, God's strength prevails. With unwavering faith and resolute perseverance, I boldly confronted the fear of failure, entrusting my journey to God's divine guidance and sovereignty.

Discovering Liberation from the Fear of Death through Eternal Hope

The fear of death, a fear shared by all humanity, was no stranger to me. The uncertainty of the unknown and the thought of parting from my loved ones loomed heavily. However, as a follower of Jesus Christ, I found solace in the promise of eternal life—a life beyond the veil of death, united eternally with my Saviour. Fixing my gaze on Jesus and the hope of heaven, I embraced liberation from the fear of death, embracing the assurance of God's unwavering love and faithfulness.

Embracing God's Promises and Letting Go of Fear's Grasp

Overcoming the spirit of fear necessitates a daily surrender to God's promises. It requires releasing our understanding and placing unwavering trust in His flawless plan for our lives. As I navigated the labyrinth of rejection, failure, and mortality, I clung to the comforting words of Isaiah 41:10, which reminded me that God stands with me, strengthening and upholding me. Casting my burdens upon Him, for He cares for me (1 Peter 5:7), I replaced fear with resolute faith in His enduring love.

Seeking God's Strength to Confront Fear Head-On

Conquering the spirit of fear calls for seeking God's strength and courage to confront it head-on. With each step of my journey, I leaned on His grace and guidance, knowing that in Him, I am more than a conqueror (Romans 8:37). Through God's unyielding love, I found the strength to stand tall against the very fears that once held me captive, allowing me to live a life of purpose, driven by faith rather than fear.

As I look back on my journey of overcoming fear, I can't help but marvel at the transformation that has taken place within me. The once all-consuming fears of rejection, failure, and death now stand defeated in the face of God's unwavering love and promises. But this victory has not come without its challenges, and I am reminded that conquering fear is an ongoing process that requires constant reliance on God's strength.

Learning to Trust in God's Plan

Throughout my journey, I have learned that fear often arises from a lack of trust in God's plan for my life. In moments of uncertainty, I would allow doubts to creep in, questioning whether God truly had good intentions for me. But as I delved deeper into His Word, I discovered the countless promises that assured me of His goodness, faithfulness, and love. Jeremiah 29:11 became a beacon of hope in my darkest moments, reminding me that God has plans to prosper me and give me a future filled with hope.

Walking in Faith, Not Sight

Overcoming fear requires walking in faith, even when circumstances seem bleak and uncertain. Like Peter stepping out of the boat to walk on water with Jesus, I have learned that it is in those moments of stepping out in faith that I experience the miraculous. Yes, there have been times when the storms of life threatened to engulf me, but just like Peter, I have found that as long as my gaze remains fixed on Jesus, fear loses its grip, and faith propels me forward.

Embracing God's Peace Amid Fear

In the face of fear, God has offered me an extraordinary gift—His peace that transcends all understanding (Philippians 4:7). It is a peace that defies logic and surpasses human comprehension. In moments of uncertainty and anxiety, I have experienced this supernatural peace enveloping my heart, reminding me that I am not alone and that God's love is greater than any fear I may encounter.

Renewing My Mind with God's Truth

To conquer fear, I have had to renew my mind daily with God's truth. Fear often feeds on negative thoughts and lies, seeking to distort my perception of God's character and intentions. But as I have replaced those lies with the truth of God's Word, fear has lost its power to manipulate my emotions and control my actions. Romans 12:2 became a guiding principle in this process, reminding me to be transformed by the renewing of my mind, so that I may discern God's will, which is good, pleasing, and perfect.

Empowered to Be a Light in the Darkness

As fear loses its grip on my life, I have discovered a newfound sense of purpose—to be a light in the darkness for others who may still be trapped in its clutches. Just as God has brought me through my fears, I now long to share the hope, peace, and love of Christ with those who are struggling. Galatians 5:13 became a calling in my heart, urging me to serve others through love and to help them break free from the chains of fear, just as I have been set free.

In Conclusion

The journey of conquering the spirit of fear has been both challenging and transformative. But through God's grace, I have been able to overcome the crippling fears that once held me captive. My life is now a testimony of God's unfailing love and power to dispel fear and replace it with faith, hope, and peace. I am forever grateful for His guidance, strength, and unwavering presence in my life, and I am committed to walking in faith, trusting in His promises, and spreading His love to a world in need of hope and freedom. As I continue to navigate life's uncertainties, I rest in the assurance that fear may knock at my door, but it will never again find a home within my heart. For in Christ, I am more than a conqueror, and through His love, I can face anything that comes my way.

CHAPTER 9: ABLAZE WITH FAITH AND LOVE – IGNITING GOD'S FIRE

Within the depths of my soul, a fire blazes—a fire ignited by the powerful forces of faith and love. This flame, not a mere metaphor but a tangible force, propels me to walk in the supernatural and embrace my role as a true and effective Christian. As I delve into the uncharted territory of faith and love, I discover the transformative power they hold—power that far exceeds my human comprehension. My journey, infused with God's Word and guided by His Spirit, unfolds with each step taken in faith.

Faith, the bedrock of my relationship with God, emerges as the assurance of things hoped for and the conviction of things unseen. As I embrace faith, I am steadfast in trusting God's promises and believing in His unending ability to exceed all expectations. My heart opens to the realm of the supernatural, where God's mighty works manifest in my life. It is through faith that I access His boundless power, recognizing that with Him, nothing is impossible.

And love—the fuel that sustains the divine flame within me —takes centre stage. Love is not a fleeting emotion but an unwavering action, selflessly and sacrificially putting others before myself, as Christ exemplified on the cross. As I walk in love, I reflect the very character of God, becoming a vessel through which, His love flows to the world. Love sets me apart as a

Christian, equipping me to leave an indelible impact on those around me.

But when faith and love unite, an undeniable synergy occurs—an ignition of God's fire within me. This fire is not one that can be contained or hidden; it is an all-consuming force, transforming me from the inside out. In its presence, doubt, fear, and unbelief melt away, replaced by boldness, confidence, and unshakable trust in God. The fire of God empowers me to transcend my human limitations and tap into the boundless resources of heaven.

As the fire of God rages within my being, I am no longer constrained by my own strength and abilities. Instead, I operate as a vessel of His power and authority. I am emboldened to step out in faith, no longer hindered by insecurity or uncertainty. The fire burns away any remnants of timidity, replacing them with unwavering assurance in God's divine guidance.

This fiery transformation empowers me to become a living testimony of God's power and grace. I now possess the tools to share the gospel with fervour and conviction, to pray with unyielding authority, and to exemplify the supernatural in my everyday life. As God's love compels me to extend compassion and healing to those in need, I find myself reaching out to the lost, embracing the unloved, and being a conduit of restoration to the hurting.

Each step I take in this journey of faith and love carries me closer to fulfilling my purpose as an agent of transformation. The world hungers for the supernatural touch of God, and my life, ablaze with faith and love, serves as a beacon of hope and light. I know that I am a vessel for God's fire to burn brightly, drawing others to Him and guiding them to the source of true life and eternal hope.

As I reflect on my journey thus far, I am filled with awe and gratitude. The fire of God's love and faith has forever changed me. It is in this holy blaze that I find the strength to navigate the challenges of life and embrace the supernatural power that surges through me. I am an ambassador of His kingdom, entrusted with this divine fire to bring forth His glory and to lead others to the everlasting truth of His Word.

So, with my heart set ablaze, I embrace the flame of God's fire within me. I walk boldly in faith, secure in the knowledge that His promises never falter. And I journey forward, enveloped in love, knowing that I am a vessel through which God's light will pierce the darkness and set captives free. May His fire forever burn within me as I press on in faith and love, fulfilling my calling as a vessel of His transformation power. For with faith, love, and the fire of God, all things are possible.

As the fire of God's love and faith continues to burn brightly within me, I am humbled by the responsibility that comes with carrying such divine power. Each day brings new opportunities to impact lives, to sow seeds of hope and truth, and to be a living testament to the miracle-working love of our Heavenly Father.

In this journey, I have encountered both triumphs and challenges. I've witnessed miracles unfold before my eyes; lives transformed by the touch of God's hand. Yet, there have been moments of doubt and uncertainty, times when the enemy seeks to quench the fiery zeal within me. But I hold steadfast to the truth that my God is greater, and His love and faithfulness endure forever.

Amid life's storms, I've learned to turn to God's Word as my compass and anchor. It is through the Scriptures that the flame within me is kindled and stoked, drawing me closer to the heart of God. The pages of the Bible hold the stories of faith-filled men and women who, through their obedience and trust in God, overcame seemingly insurmountable obstacles.

The lives of Abraham, Moses, David, and countless others inspire me to embrace the power of faith. These heroes of faith dared to believe in the impossible, and in doing so, they set in motion a chain of events that reshaped history. Their unwavering trust in God's promises has ignited the spark of determination within me. If they could conquer giants, part seas, and move mountains, then surely, with the same God, I can face any challenge that lies ahead.

Moreover, I am reminded of the greatest demonstration of love—the sacrifice of Jesus on the cross. His selfless act was the ultimate manifestation of love, a love that redeems and reconciles, a love that brings hope to the hopeless and light to the darkness. His love knows no bounds, reaching even the depths of our brokenness, restoring us and empowering us to love others as He loves us.

As I continue on this journey, I am acutely aware of the impact my life can have on others. Every word spoken, every act of kindness, and every demonstration of faith and love can plant seeds of transformation in the hearts of those I encounter. It is not my strength that makes a difference but the power of God's fire working through me.

I am determined to fan the flames of this divine fire through prayer, worship, and daily surrender to God's will. My heart longs for more of Him, and I yearn to be a vessel through which His love and power flow freely. I seek to be sensitive to the Holy Spirit's leading, knowing that He will guide me to those who need to experience the fire of God's love and healing.

In this pursuit of faith and love, I am not alone. I am part of a global community of believers, each one with their unique calling and purpose. Together, we form a mighty army, marching forward in unity, driven by love, and propelled by faith. Our mission is to spread the flame of God's fire to every corner of the earth, leaving no soul untouched by His transforming love.

With hearts ablaze, we press on, fuelled by the knowledge that God's fire is limitless, unquenchable, and ever-expanding. The world may try to extinguish it, but it will never succeed. The flame of God's love and faith will continue to burn brightly, illuminating the darkest places and drawing people into the warmth of His embrace.

As I conclude this chapter, I am overwhelmed with gratitude for the privilege of being a carrier of God's fire. It is not a burden but a divine honour to walk in faith and love, fuelled by His power. I rest assured that as long as I remain in His presence, seeking His face, and trusting in His unfailing love, this fire will continue to burn brightly within me, illuminating my path and impacting the lives of those I encounter.

With each step forward, I embrace the fire of God's love and faith. I am determined to ignite a blaze that will not be contained but will spread far and wide, setting the world ablaze with the transformative power of the Almighty. Together, let us continue to walk in faith and love, igniting the fire of God's presence wherever we go. For in His love and faith, we find the strength to overcome, the power to impact lives, and the hope to change the world.

CHAPTER 10: BREAKING FREE FROM UNFORGIVENESS – EMBRACING HEALING AND WHOLENESS

The weight of unforgiveness is an insidious burden that can wreak havoc on every aspect of our lives. As I reflect on the detrimental effects of holding onto grudges and resentments, I am reminded of the profound wisdom in the teachings of Jesus. His words in Matthew 6:14-15 resonate deeply within me, urging me to release the shackles of unforgiveness so that I may experience the fullness of God's forgiveness and healing.

Physically, the toll of unforgiveness is evident. The toxic emotions that brew within us when we refuse to forgive can manifest in various health issues. Stress, anger, and bitterness act as silent enemies, undermining our well-being and making us vulnerable to ailments such as high blood pressure, heart disease, and even cancer. The wisdom found in Proverbs 14:30 rings true as I realize that peace in our hearts can breathe life into our bodies, while envy and resentment corrode us from within.

Psychologically, unforgiveness takes a toll on our mental health, robbing us of the joy and peace we so desperately seek. The incessant replaying of past hurts traps us in a negative cycle, fostering feelings of anxiety, paranoia, and depression. As I ponder the wise counsel of the apostle Paul in Philippians 4:8, I am reminded of the power of shifting our focus toward the positive aspects of life. Choosing to forgive allows us to break free from the mental prison of unforgiveness and opens the door to healing and emotional well-being.

Spiritually, the impact of unforgiveness is profound and far-reaching. By holding onto grudges, we inadvertently give the devil a foothold in our lives, allowing darkness to encroach upon our souls. Ephesians 4:26-27 serves as a sobering reminder that unforgiveness weakens our spiritual defences and exposes us to the enemy's attacks. To align ourselves with the redemptive power of God, we must heed the advice of Jesus in Luke 6:37, which urges us to forgive, thereby breaking free from the destructive influence of unforgiveness.

Breaking the chains of unforgiveness is not an option; it is a commandment from our Saviour. As I meditate on these truths, I am filled with a newfound resolve to embrace the power of forgiveness. Choosing to forgive is not a sign of weakness, but an act of obedience and surrender to God's will. It is through this transformative act that we pave the way for God's grace and mercy to flow abundantly into our lives.

In conclusion, the detrimental effects of unforgiveness are undeniable. They corrode our physical health, sap our mental strength, and weaken us spiritually. However, by heeding the teachings of Jesus and embracing the power of forgiveness, we unlock the door to healing and wholeness in every dimension of our being.

Let us choose to forgive, not just once, but as an ongoing lifestyle. In doing so, we release the burdens that weigh us down and embrace the freedom that comes with forgiveness. As we walk in forgiveness, we experience the transformative power of God's love, which restores, heals, and sets us on a path of peace and reconciliation. May the flame of forgiveness burn brightly within our hearts, illuminating the way to a life of true well-being and abundance in Christ.

As I reflect on the path to breaking free from the chains of unforgiveness, I am reminded of the importance of taking practical steps toward healing and reconciliation. While the decision to forgive is a powerful starting point, the journey toward wholeness requires intentionality and perseverance.

One of the first steps on this journey is to confront the pain and hurt caused by the offence. Acknowledging our emotions and bringing them before God in prayer allows us to process the hurt in a healthy way. Psalm 34:18 assures us that "The Lord is close to the broken-hearted and saves those who are crushed in spirit." In His presence, we find comfort and strength to face our wounds and begin the process of healing.

Next, we must choose to extend forgiveness to those who have wronged us. It may not be easy, and the wounds might still feel fresh, but embracing the words of Colossians 3:13 becomes paramount: "Bear with each other and forgive one another if any of you has a grievance against someone. Forgive as the Lord forgave you." As we remember the magnitude of God's forgiveness towards us, we find the courage to forgive others.

However, forgiveness does not always mean condoning the hurtful actions or restoring a broken relationship. In cases where reconciliation is not possible or safe, it is crucial to set healthy boundaries and seek support from trusted friends, family, or professional counsellors. Proverbs 27:17 reminds us, "As iron sharpens iron, so one person sharpens another." Engaging in open dialogue and seeking wise counsel can provide valuable insights on the path to healing.

Additionally, we must also remember to forgive ourselves. Often, we carry the weight of self-condemnation and guilt for past mistakes, preventing us from embracing God's grace fully. Accepting God's forgiveness and allowing ourselves to move forward is an essential step in experiencing complete freedom.

Throughout this journey, prayer becomes our lifeline. Consistent communication with God invites His guidance, strength, and healing power into our lives. We can trust that God will lead us toward a place of restoration and peace as we seek Him diligently.

Walking the path of forgiveness is not without its challenges, but it is a journey worth taking. As I strive to embrace the transformative power of forgiveness in my own life, I am filled with a newfound sense of hope and liberation. The detrimental effects of unforgiveness are no longer an overwhelming force, for the love and grace of God are more potent.

In conclusion, the journey to break free from the detrimental effects of unforgiveness is an opportunity for profound growth and healing. It involves facing our pain, choosing to forgive, setting healthy boundaries, seeking support, forgiving ourselves, and leaning on the power of prayer. As we embrace forgiveness as a lifestyle, we become agents of reconciliation, spreading the love and grace of God to a world desperately in need of healing. Let us walk this path hand in hand with our Saviour, trusting in His wisdom and grace to lead us toward a life of true freedom and wholeness.

CHAPTER 11: THE NEED FOR SPIRITUAL DELIVERANCE

As I ponder the importance of spiritual deliverance, I am humbled by the realization that our fast-paced world is not immune to the influence of spiritual forces, both positive and negative. The Bible's wisdom provides us with guidance on navigating these unseen realms and seeking deliverance based on godly principles to safeguard our lives from darkness.

A fundamental step in our pursuit of spiritual deliverance is to distance ourselves from anything related to the dark arts, such as witchcraft or occult practices. These activities are unequivocally condemned in Scripture, as they seek supernatural power outside of God's divine plan. Deuteronomy 18:10-12 explicitly warns against such practices, revealing that they are an abomination to the Lord.

Yet, avoidance alone may not be enough. Sometimes, we unknowingly fall prey to spiritual bondage that can manifest in various distressing ways, like oppression, depression, addictions, or unexplained physical ailments. When faced with such challenges, seeking spiritual deliverance becomes vital.

Deliverance can take various forms, tailored to address individual needs. It may involve the casting out of demonic influences, breaking generational curses that have plagued families, or denouncing altars that we have unwittingly submitted to. These altars often represent false gods or idols that have drawn our attention and devotion away from the one true God.

The Bible is a testament to the potency of deliverance and the authority bestowed upon believers to confront spiritual strongholds. Jesus, during His earthly ministry, performed numerous deliverances, freeing people from demonic oppression and restoring them to wholeness. As stated in Luke 4:18, He declared His anointing to proclaim liberty to the captives and recovery of sight to the blind.

We, as believers, have been graced with the same authority through the indwelling of the Holy Spirit. The apostle Paul reaffirms this in Ephesians 6:12, emphasizing that our battle is not against flesh and blood but against spiritual forces of evil. This understanding empowers us to stand firm against the darkness, knowing that we have divine authority to overcome any spiritual opposition.

In conclusion, recognizing the need for spiritual deliverance is an essential aspect of our faith journey. We must adhere to biblical principles and abstain from any involvement in dark practices. Moreover, we may find ourselves in need of deliverance from spiritual bondages, which can entail casting out demons, breaking generational curses, and denouncing altars that have held us captive. Let us be encouraged, for as believers, we possess the authority and power of Jesus Christ, who has set us free from all spiritual strongholds. With hearts open to God's guidance, may we continue to walk in His light and experience the liberating force of spiritual deliverance in every aspect of our lives.

CHAPTER 12: GO FOR BIBLICAL COUNSELLING

Introduction:

In the journey of life, we all encounter challenges that can leave us feeling overwhelmed and in need of guidance. As a believer, I know the significance of seeking counsel that aligns with my faith and values. In this chapter, we will delve into the importance of finding professional Christian counsellors who can provide guidance using the timeless wisdom of God's Word.

The Danger of Secular Counsel:

When seeking counsel, I have learned to be cautious about the source and perspective of the advice I receive. Secular counsel, though well-intentioned, may lack the spiritual foundation needed to address the root causes of my struggles. It can inadvertently lead me away from my Christian faith and add to my confusion. (Psalm 1:1-2)

The Power of Biblical Counselling:

On the other hand, I have come to appreciate the power of biblical counselling. It relies on the profound wisdom and truth found in the Scriptures, acknowledging that God's Word holds the answers to my deepest questions and provides guidance for every aspect of my life. By seeking counsel grounded in the Bible, I allow God's truth to shape my perspectives and actions, leading to lasting transformation. (2 Timothy 3:16-17)

Finding Professional Christian Counsellors:

In my quest for effective biblical counselling, I have understood the importance of seeking out qualified Christian counsellors. These professionals possess a solid understanding of the Scriptures and the principles of Christian living. They are uniquely equipped to help me navigate through the challenges I face, providing guidance based on the unchanging truth of God's Word. (Proverbs 11:14)

The Role of Faith and Prayer:

As I embark on the journey of biblical counselling, I know that approaching it with faith and a humble heart is crucial. I recognize that true healing and transformation come from God, and I must willingly submit myself to His guidance and rely on His strength to overcome the obstacles in my life. Prayer becomes an integral part of the counselling process, seeking God's wisdom, discernment, and intervention. (James 5:13-16)

The Benefits of Biblical Counselling:

Embracing biblical counselling has brought tremendous benefits into my life. I have experienced healing, restoration, and renewed hope. It goes beyond addressing my immediate concerns; it equips me with timeless tools and principles that will guide me throughout my life's journey. With God's Word as my guide, I am confident that I can face life's challenges and emerge stronger. (Psalm 32:8)

Conclusion:

In conclusion, seeking biblical counselling is an indispensable aspect of my life as a believer. By avoiding secular counsel and embracing the wisdom of God's Word, I position myself to experience true transformation and restoration. I hold on to the truth that God's Word is a lamp unto my feet and a light unto my path, providing the guidance and counsel I need to navigate life's challenges with unwavering faith. (Psalm 119:105) With God's Word as my anchor, I am confident that I can face any trial that comes my way. As believers, let us wholeheartedly embrace biblical counselling and allow God's truth to illuminate our paths, leading us to a life of healing, growth, and purpose.

CHAPTER 13: EMBRACING THE BLESSINGS OF CHURCH AND PASTORAL COVERING

As I reflect on my journey of faith, I cannot emphasize enough the significance of finding a church home and a pastoral covering. It is a decision that has transformed my life, providing me with a sense of belonging, guidance, and spiritual growth. In this chapter, I want to delve into the profound benefits of having a church community and a pastoral covering, as well as shed light on the potential disadvantages of not having one. Let us seek wisdom and understanding from the Scriptures to reinforce these truths.

Fellowship and Support: The Power of Community

The church community is a haven of fellowship, support, and encouragement in our walk with Christ. Hebrews 10:24-25 resonates deeply within me, "And let us consider how to stir up one another to love and good works, not neglecting to meet together, as is the habit of some, but encouraging one another, and all the more as you see the Day drawing near." As I became a part of a church, I experienced the beauty of building meaningful relationships and finding support in times of need. Together, we spur one another on toward love and good deeds, knowing that we are not alone on this journey.

Spiritual Nourishment: Feasting on God's Word

In the church, I found a platform for spiritual nourishment through the powerful combination of preaching, teaching, and worship. The truth in 2 Timothy 3:16-17 resonates deeply within me, "All Scripture is breathed out by God and profitable for teaching, for reproof, for correction, and for training in righteousness, that the man of God may be complete, equipped for every good work." Attending church regularly has allowed me to receive the Word of God, which guides and equips me for my journey of faith. It is through this nourishment that I have grown in wisdom and understanding, seeking to live a life that honours Him.

Accountability and Discipleship: Thriving under Pastoral Guidance

Having a pastoral covering has been an incredible blessing, ensuring accountability and discipleship in my life. 1 Peter 5:2-3 echoes in my heart, "Shepherd the flock of God that is among you, exercising oversight, not under compulsion, but willingly, as God would have you; not for shameful gain, but eagerly; not domineering over those in your charge, but being examples to the flock." Under the guidance of a pastor, I have received wisdom, correction, and mentorship, which has strengthened my faith and helped me navigate life's challenges with integrity. I am grateful for their leadership and care, for they have been living examples of Christ's love.

The Disadvantages of Not Having a Church Community

Isolation and Lack of Support: A Lonely Journey

I have come to understand that without a church community, isolation and lack of support can be disheartening. Ecclesiastes

4:9-10 serves as a sobering reminder, "Two are better than one because they have a good reward for their toil. For if they fall, one will lift up his fellow. But woe to him who is alone when he falls and has not another to lift him up!" Being part of a church family means we can lean on one another during challenging times and share in the joys of life together. Together, we find strength in unity.

Spiritual Stagnation: Missing Out on Growth

Not being connected to a church community can lead to spiritual stagnation. In 2 Peter 3:18, Peter urges believers to "grow in the grace and knowledge of our Lord and Saviour Jesus Christ." A church community provides ample opportunities for growth, learning, and the development of spiritual gifts. When we are nourished by the Word and surrounded by fellow believers, we are better equipped to mature as disciples of Christ.

Lack of Accountability: Straying from the Path

Proverbs 27:17 serves as a poignant reminder, "Iron sharpens iron, and one man sharpens another." Without a pastoral covering, we may lack the necessary accountability to stay on the right path. A pastor serves as a guide, providing wisdom, correction, and accountability, helping us navigate the challenges and temptations of life with steadfastness.

In Conclusion: Embracing the Fullness of God's Plan

In conclusion, I wholeheartedly affirm the importance of finding a church home and embracing a pastoral covering. The benefits of church community, including fellowship, support, spiritual nourishment, accountability, and discipleship, are clearly outlined in the Scriptures. On the other hand, the disadvantages of not having a church community, such as isolation, spiritual stagnation, and lack of accountability, can hinder our growth and well-being.

Let us seek a church home and humbly embrace the pastoral covering that God has ordained for us. As we do so, we position ourselves to experience the fullness of God's plan for our lives. With God's Word as our guide and the support of our church family, we can navigate life's challenges with unwavering faith. Let us be grateful for the blessings of church and pastoral covering, knowing that they are vital for our spiritual journey and growth.

CHAPTER 14: UNLEASHING THE POWER OF PRAYER AND FASTING

As I navigate through the challenges and trials of this world as a believer, I am acutely aware of the constant battle against unseen forces. Spiritual warfare rages on, with temptations from the enemy and the struggles of my own flesh seeking to hinder my faith and purpose. In this chapter, I am eager to explore the transformative impact of leading a prayerful and fasted life, recognizing the effectiveness of these spiritual disciplines in equipping me for the battles I face.

The Scriptures resound with the truth that our fight is not against mere mortal beings but against rulers, authorities, cosmic powers over this present darkness, and spiritual forces of evil in the heavenly realms (Ephesians 6:12). These adversaries relentlessly seek to steal, kill, and destroy our faith, relationships, and destinies. Thankfully, as children of God, we are not left defenceless. He has bestowed upon us powerful weapons to combat these forces, and prayer and fasting are among the most potent tools at our disposal.

Prayer stands as our direct line of communication with God, our Father. It is a sacred channel through which we pour out our deepest desires, fears, and needs to Him. No mere religious ritual, prayer embodies a heartfelt conversation with the Creator of the universe. When I pray, I invite God into my situations, requesting His divine intervention, guidance, and protection. Through prayer, I find solace, comfort, and strength to bravely confront the battles ahead.

Fasting, a spiritual discipline involving abstaining from food for a specific time, transcends mere physical abstinence. Rather, it holds profound spiritual implications. Fasting becomes a means to deny my fleshly desires and focus my attention wholly on God. Throughout history, believers have practiced fasting as a means of humbling themselves before God, seeking His face, and consecrating themselves for spiritual breakthroughs. It becomes an act of self-discipline, enabling me to overcome worldly distractions and draw nearer to God.

The words of Jesus in Matthew 17:21 echo the significance of prayer and fasting in confronting spiritual battles: "But this kind does not go out except by prayer and fasting." Together, they form a powerful combination, unlocking the supernatural realm and unleashing God's power in our lives. Prayer and fasting align our hearts with God's will, allowing Him to work in and through us, empowering us to overcome the challenges that confront us.

Throughout the Scriptures, we encounter numerous examples of individuals who sought God through these spiritual disciplines and experienced divine breakthroughs. From Moses, who fasted for forty days and received the Ten Commandments, to Daniel, praying and fasting for twenty-one days and gaining divine wisdom, the power of prayer and fasting is vividly evident. Jesus Himself serves as the ultimate model, dedicating extended periods of prayer and fasting to prepare for His divine mission.

In conclusion, as believers facing relentless battles, leading a prayerful and fasted life becomes paramount. Prayer and fasting are not mere religious observances but rather powerful spiritual disciplines that equip us to face the trials ahead. Through prayer, we invite God into our situations, seeking His guidance and protection. Fasting humbles our hearts, drawing us nearer to God and opening the door for His supernatural intervention. Embracing the importance of a prayerful and fasted life, we triumph over the battles before us, living victoriously in Christ.

CHAPTER 15: WHY I CHOSE GRACE - EMBRACING GOD'S UNCONDITIONAL LOVE

As I reflect on my journey, I find myself overwhelmed by the profound realisation that God's grace has been the defining factor in my life. Grace, bestowed upon us through Jesus Christ's finished work on the cross, is the very essence of God's unconditional love for humanity. It is a gift that extends far beyond our own efforts or merits, a gift that has the power to transform lives and offers hope to the broken-hearted.

The journey of discovering grace began when I recognized that my own works and efforts could never truly satisfy the longing in my soul. I once sought fulfilment through self-reliance and achievements, but in my pursuit of perfection, I only found a sense of emptiness and weariness. It was during one of my lowest moments that I encountered the overwhelming truth of God's grace, which became my lifeline and refuge.

In the scriptures, we find a profound testament to God's merciful nature and his tender care for the broken hearted. Psalm 34:18 (NIV) reassures us that "The Lord is close to the broken hearted and saves those who are crushed in spirit." In my moments of despair, it was the unwavering love of God that lifted me up, offering solace to my weary heart and healing to my wounded soul. It was through His grace that I discovered that my brokenness did not disqualify me from His love but, in fact, made me a prime recipient of His boundless compassion.

Choosing grace meant acknowledging my limitations and embracing the truth that it is through Christ's finished work on the cross that I find salvation and redemption. In Ephesians 2:8-9 (NIV), it is written, "For it is by grace you have been saved, through faith—and this is not from yourselves, it is the gift of God—not by works so that no one can boast." It was a humbling realization that my own efforts could not earn me salvation, but God's grace freely offered it to me as an unmerited gift.

Embracing grace has also brought me closer to the realization of God's loving provision. He has given us the Holy Spirit as our Helper, our Comforter, and our Guide. In John 14:26 (NIV), Jesus promised, "But the Advocate, the Holy Spirit, whom the Father will send in my name, will teach you all things and will remind you of everything I have said to you." The Holy Spirit, an indwelling presence, empowers us in all situations, equipping us with divine wisdom and strength.

It is through this divine assistance that I have found solace during life's storms and wisdom in moments of uncertainty. The Holy Spirit has been my guiding light, leading me through the darkest valleys and rejoicing with me in moments of triumph. The knowledge that I am not alone but have the Spirit of God residing within me has provided an unshakable foundation of confidence and assurance.

In conclusion, my choice to embrace grace has transformed my life and redefined my understanding of God's love. I have experienced the boundless compassion of a merciful God who reaches out to the broken-hearted and offers His unconditional love to all who humbly seek Him. Through the finished work of Jesus Christ on the cross, I have found my true help and salvation. The Holy Spirit, my constant companion, empowers me to navigate life's challenges and embrace the abundant life that God has planned for me.

Choosing grace is not a one-time decision but a lifelong journey of surrendering to God's love and embracing His unmerited favour. It is my hope that by sharing this chapter, others may also come to recognize the transformative power of grace and experience the fullness of God's love in their own lives.

Conclusion: Transformed by Grace: A Journey of Faith and Love

In this reflective tale, I share the profound and transformative journey of my life, infused with faith, and guided by love. Growing up in a devout Christian family in Jamaica, I cherished the warmth of faith as an integral part of my being. Nevertheless, my path was not without challenges, and in high school, I found myself grappling with darkness and despair.

A pivotal moment came when I decided to migrate to England, a choice that caused me to drift away from my faith, burdened by struggles that seemed insurmountable. But in an act of divine intervention, God brought a remarkable woman into my life, reigniting the embers of my faith. In a touching visitation, I felt the presence of the Almighty Himself, igniting a passionate fire within me.

From that moment on, I devoted my life to spreading the love and healing power of Jesus. As the shepherd of Christ Liquid Fire Ministry in London, I became a vessel for God's awe-inspiring miracles, signs, and wonders. Witnessing brokenness healed, depression lifted, and afflictions cast away, I experienced firsthand the incredible potency of Jesus' love.

My life bears testimony to the boundless mercy and love of Jesus. It is a story of hope triumphing over darkness, and it calls out to all to embrace the all-encompassing grace that surrounds us. Through these profound experiences, I have learned that divine grace holds the extraordinary power to transform lives and challenge the very fabric of our perceptions.

In closing, I extend my heartfelt gratitude to all those who have been a part of this remarkable journey. To my cherished family, friends, and mentors, your unwavering love and encouragement have been my guiding light. To the remarkable woman who led me back to God, you are a beacon of divine grace.

And above all, I offer my deepest thanks to Jesus, whose infinite mercy and love have been the cornerstone of this incredible transformation. Without Him, I would not have experienced the life-changing metamorphosis that now defines me. Forever grateful for His presence and the indomitable power of His love, I stand as a testament to the journey of faith, love, and grace.

Acknowledgements: A Journey of Gratitude and Blessings

In this remarkable journey of faith and love, I have been surrounded by a tapestry of incredible individuals whose unwavering support and love have shaped my life in profound ways. It is with the deepest sense of gratitude that I acknowledge and honour these exceptional souls, whose presence has been a true blessing.

First and foremost, I express heartfelt thanks to my mom and dad, who have set the standard for Godly living. Their unyielding faith and love for Jesus have been a beacon of inspiration and guidance throughout my life. I am truly blessed to have been raised by such amazing parents, and their unwavering devotion has instilled in me a foundation of strength and spirituality that has sustained me through the years.

Acknowledgement

To my beloved wife, the epitome of kindness and devotion, you are not only my life partner but also my rock and support. Your love and encouragement have carried me through the darkest of times and propelled my spiritual growth to new heights. I thank God each day for bringing you into my life, for you are a precious gift from above.

To my dear daughter, who has forever changed my world, thank you for infusing my life with immeasurable joy and purpose. Your innocent and pure love serves as a constant reminder of God's boundless and unconditional love for all of us. You are a cherished blessing from God, and I am eternally grateful for the privilege of being your parent.

To my extended circle of friends and family, you have been the pillars of strength and solace during both triumphs and trials. Your unwavering presence and outpouring of love and support have been nothing short of invaluable. I give thanks to God for placing each and every one of you in my life, as your presence has enriched my journey beyond measure.

Above all, I offer profound thanks to the Almighty God, whose infinite mercy and grace have been the guiding force behind this entire expedition. Without His divine guidance and intervention, I would not have reached this point in my journey. He has lovingly carried me through trials and tribulations, and his boundless love has transformed my life in ways I could never have imagined.

To all those who have played a part in shaping my journey, no matter how big or small, I extend my deepest gratitude from the bottom of my heart. Your love, prayers, and support have been the lifeblood of my endeavours, and I pray that God continues to abundantly bless each one of you.

In closing, I stand humbled and grateful for the remarkable individuals who have graced my life with their presence. To each person who has contributed to this journey of gratitude and blessings, you have my eternal appreciation. May God's love and favour be poured upon you, guiding you always in the path of light and joy.

Printed in Great Britain
by Amazon

25928859R00036